Do I Have To?

Kids Talk About Responsibility

Written by
Nancy Loewen

Illustrated by
Omarr Wesley

Content Adviser: Lorraine O. Moore, Ph.D., Educational Psychology
Reading Adviser: Lauren A. Liang, M.A., Literacy Education, University of Minnesota

PICTURE WINDOW BOOKS
Minneapolis, Minnesota

Editor: Nadia Higgins
Designer: Thomas Emery
Page production: Picture Window Books
The illustrations in this book were prepared digitally.

Picture Window Books
1710 Roe Crest Drive
North Mankato, MN 56003
www.capstonepub.com

Library of Congress Cataloging-in-Publication Data
Loewen, Nancy, 1964–
  Do I have to? : kids talk about responsibility / written by Nancy Loewen ;
illustrated by Omarr Wesley.
     p. cm. Includes index.
  Summary: Uses an advice-column format to define responsibility as a character
value and demonstrate how it can be used in daily situations.
     ISBN 978-1-4048-0030-4 (hardcover)
     ISBN 978-1-4048-0363-3 (paperback)
  1. Responsibility in children—Juvenile literature. [1. Responsibility.]
I. Wesley, Omarr, ill. II. Title.
  HQ772.5 .L64 2003
  302.3'2—dc21
                                                        2002005987

Printed in the United States 5702

To my children,
Louis and Helena—
always my best teachers

Hi! I'm Tina Truly. You can call me T. Welcome to my very own advice column. That means kids write to me about their problems, and I give them ideas about how to fix them. Check it out!

Just so you know, I'm 13 years old. I live with my dad and stepmom and big brother, Josh. I'm in the seventh grade at Meandering Middle School. My professional credentials include:

- reading "Dear Abby" in the newspaper since I was nine.
- parents who do a pretty good job of explaining things (although sometimes they make *no* sense whatsoever).
- a habit of sticking my nose in other people's business. (But, hey, this column lets me get it out of my system without bugging anybody.)

Today's column is about responsibility. That means taking care of things, keeping your word, being reliable—all that stuff. It can get really tough sometimes. So send in your letters. I'll be waiting!

Sincerely,

Tina Truly

Dear T. Truly:

I want a dog more than anything, but my mom won't let me have one. She says it's because of what happened to my hamster. (Long story. Let's just say that the house is starting to smell better now.) What can I do so my mom will let me have a dog?

Petless in Pittsburgh

Dear Petless:

My family has a dog. He's a boxer named Ali. He's great, but lots of work. We have to feed him and brush him and take him to the vet. If we go on vacation, we have to find a place for him. We have to walk him twice a day, even if it's pouring rain or five degrees below zero. We even have to clean up his you-know-what.

When we first got Ali, my stepmom took care of all that stuff. It was great. Then she got fed up. She said if Josh and Dad and I didn't start pulling our weight, she'd start looking for a new home for Ali. So we set up a schedule and put it on the fridge, and now everyone pitches in. Even Dad.

Sounds like you've already figured out something about pet ownership. (What DID happen to that hamster, anyway?) My advice is, if you really want a dog, you'll need to show your mom that you mean business. Do a great job with your other chores so she'll see how responsible you can be. You could also try making a chart of dog chores and a schedule that shows when you'd do them. Maybe she'll change her mind after all.

But even if you turn into The Most Wonderful Kid in the World, she might still say no. Getting a dog is a big deal for the whole family. Try not to bug her. It's weird, but bugging can turn a perfectly good parent into a real crab—and I don't think that's the sort of pet you had in mind.

Take care, Petless!

T. Truly

8

Hi, Tina.

I've got homework troubles. Either I forget to do it, or I forget it at home. And sometimes it just disappears. What can I do?

Jeanette

Dear Jeanette:

Wow, do I know about this one! I hate to break it to you, but homework doesn't get any easier as you get older. I've got homework in just about every subject, just about every night. It's a good thing I've got one of those backpacks with wheels.

Anyway, to help me keep track of it all, I keep a special notebook. I write down all my assignments and when they're due. (Plus I add notes about the advice I'd like to give my teachers, but that's just me.) I try to do my homework at the same time every day. (My stepmom came up with that idea.) As soon as I'm done, I put the homework in my backpack so my dog Ali doesn't eat it.

Some of my friends have other ways of dealing with homework. Trish and Val call each other every night to make sure they remembered stuff right. Brad does his homework the minute he gets home from school, while it's still fresh in his mind. Jeremy's lucky—if he does all his homework on time, his parents add some bonus money to his allowance!

My point is, every kid has a different strategy. If you and your parents do some brainstorming, I'll bet you can come up with a plan that works for you. Hang in there!

T. Truly

P.S. If these ideas don't help, you could try the Memory Magician. I saw it advertised on TV. It's only three easy payments of $19.95—guaranteed to work or your money back. (And if it works, let me know. I know a few people who could really use it.)

Dear T. Truly:

I'm really mad at Ted, who USED to be my best friend. He's totally irresponsible. He said he'd help me make posters for our baseball team's car wash, but then he never even showed up. He said he'd trade his glow-in-the-dark warthog for my glow-in-the-dark platypus, but then he went off and traded with Andy instead. He borrowed my Deranged Dinosaurs computer game two months ago, and I haven't seen it since. Should I give up on him and find a new best friend?

Frustrated in Fairbanks

Dear Frustrated:

Sorry, Frustrated, I can't answer your question. Only you can. What does Ted mean to you? Are you better off with him or without him? The only thing I know for sure is, don't make up your mind too quickly. This is a big deal.

Have you ever told Ted how you feel when he breaks his promises? Maybe he doesn't even know. Even me. Like, a few months ago, my friend Sally was mad at me because I was late once or twice meeting her at the mall. (Okay, it was more like three times.) I had no idea it even bothered her. When she finally told me how annoyed she was, I felt pretty bad. But we're over it now, and I'm hardly ever late anymore.

Hope this helps, Frustrated.

T. Truly

Dear T.:

I've got some major scheduling problems. This Thursday I've got a dance recital AND a piano recital. I'll have to miss my You-Can-Speak-Spanish field trip on Friday so I can be in a karate tournament. Then I'm going camping with my Girls Explore troop over the weekend. AND I've got a book report due next Monday. Help me, Tina!

Whirlwind Wendy

12

Dear Whirlwind:

My brother, Josh, went through something like that. He played basketball, had the lead in a school play, took guitar lessons, was in the church youth group, and some other stuff, too. He was so busy he hardly ever had time to just hang out with us. (And he was being such a grump, I didn't want him around anyway.)

When Josh came home with a rotten report card, my dad and stepmom said he had to drop some activities. They said he had to pick his favorites—only one or two—and he could do the other stuff later. He was mad at first, but after a while he said he was glad he wasn't stuck in the car all the time, eating his supper from his lap. Now he's a lot nicer—most of the time. And there aren't nearly as many ketchup stains in the car.

If I were you, I'd be too tired to even write this letter. Maybe you want to drop something. I mean, it's not like you won't have a few years left to get the other stuff in. My uncle started taking karate when he was ancient—40! My mom's playing soccer with her girlfriends on Wednesday nights. Weird, but true. So, take it easy, Whirlwind.

T. Truly

Dear T.:

Rules, rules, rules! Every time I turn around it's "Clean up your room" or "Hang up your coat" or "You can't eat that in here." Who cares if the house is a little messy? Life's too short!

A Proud Member of the United Slobs of America

16

Dear Proud:

I know how you feel. I've got some clean-room issues going on these days, too. I'm still working at it, but for now let me ask you a few questions, adapted from my dad's Lecture Number 57.

1. Do you waste a lot of time trying to find things?
2. When you do finally clean up, do you find cool stuff you'd forgotten about?
3. Do you ever step on things and break them—or hurt yourself? (Dad's real sensitive about that one. He's still got a scar on his foot from stepping on the Mini Mighty Mangler action figure my brother left in the middle of the floor five years ago.)
4. Do your family members get all cranky from picking up after you?

If you answered yes to any of these questions, you might want to think more about the rules at your house. Like Dad says, sometimes rules are there for a reason.

Dad sure lectures a lot, but I have to admit, once in a while he comes up with an okay idea. Like cleaning my room a little bit three times a week instead of a lot once a week. That way it's not so discouraging. He goes on about how breaking up a big job into little pieces makes everything easier. And if I get through 30 days in a row without leaving crumbs in the den, I get to pick out a new CD. (I'm on Day 12. So far, so good!) Maybe your parents would go for something like that, too. It's worth a try. Life's too short to be arguing all the time.

T. Truly

Dear T. Truly:

I'm writing about my friend Scott. His dad has been really sick, and Scott seems sad and worried all the time. What can I do to help?

Ben from Georgia

Dear Ben:

This is a tough question, for sure. But I think the best thing you can do for Scott is to keep on being his friend. When my parents got divorced four years ago, my whole life changed, and I felt bad for a long time. But I still remember how my friends Jenny and Brian would try to cheer me up.

Jenny invited me over to her house on Friday nights, and she let me pick out the movie every single time. She even let me sleep with her cat. Brian sat with me on the bus and told me so many dumb jokes I just had to laugh. Those guys really made me feel better. And you can do the same for Scott. You probably won't be able to do anything about his situation, but at least you can let him know he can count on you. You'd be surprised how much it means when someone reaches out a helping hand.

Good luck, Ben!

T. Truly

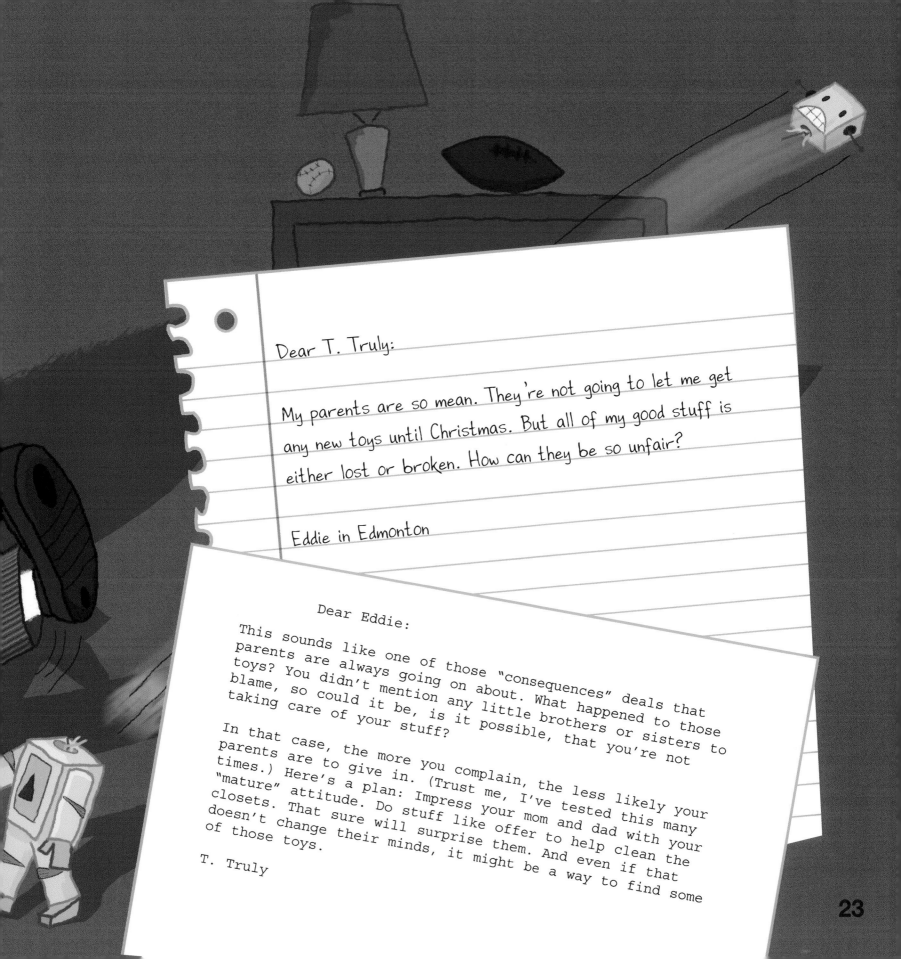

Dear T. Truly:

My parents are so mean. They're not going to let me get any new toys until Christmas. But all of my good stuff is either lost or broken. How can they be so unfair?

Eddie in Edmonton

Dear Eddie:

This sounds like one of those "consequences" deals that parents are always going on about. What happened to those toys? You didn't mention any little brothers or sisters to blame, so could it be, is it possible, that you're not taking care of your stuff?

In that case, the more you complain, the less likely your parents are to give in. (Trust me, I've tested this many times.) Here's a plan: Impress your mom and dad with your "mature" attitude. Do stuff like offer to help clean the closets. That sure will surprise them. And even if that doesn't change their minds, it might be a way to find some of those toys.

T. Truly

Hi, T.

My mom works a lot, so she makes me do lots of things around the house. I have to help my sister get ready in the mornings and watch her after school. I have to make breakfast and pack our lunches. I do a lot of cleaning, too. Sometimes I get mad at my mom because it just doesn't seem fair that I have to do so much.

Overworked and Underpaid

Dear Overworked:

This is another tough one. Maybe it will help to know that you're not alone, even if it feels that way sometimes. A lot of kids are in the same boat that you are in. My friend Lana has to watch not one, not two, but THREE little brothers after school. (She knows how to get gum out of hair, how to unplug a toilet, how to get little kids to eat their vegetables, and lots of other things.)

Your mom probably wishes she could be home more. After all, it's not like she's out playing golf and getting her nails done all day long. She's working so you can have the things you need.

I bet if the two of you put your heads together, you could come up with ways to make it easier. Maybe a friend could come over to help you. Or maybe there's an older kid in your neighborhood, or even a nice grandparent-type person, who could babysit your sister once in a while or help with the cleaning.

But the most important thing is, you've got to talk to your mom and tell her how you feel. Make some time for each other, even if it's just for a good tickle session or a quick game of Go Fish. If you feel good about each other, the bad stuff won't seem so bad. That's what Lana says, and she's one of the smartest people I know.

T. Truly

Hey there, T. Truly.

I have a story that could save your readers a lot of trouble. One day, I started to bike over to my friend Jason's house. It was just a few blocks away, so I didn't think I needed to wear my helmet. Well, I swerved to avoid hitting a caterpillar (one of those brown, fuzzy ones) and crashed big time. I ended up in the hospital for two weeks. I missed out on our class field trip to Reptile City and lots of other fun things. Please tell your readers to wear a helmet when they're biking or skating. Save your brains!

Numbskull No More

PRESS

Dear Numbskull No More:

Thanks for your letter. I hope that caterpillar knows how lucky it was!

To all my readers: being a responsible person means taking good care of yourself, too. That's what my dad says. Here are some quotes from his Lecture Number 12:

- Wear your helmets and your seatbelts.
- Eat stuff that's good for you.
- Exercise a little every day.
- Get enough sleep.
- If you need help with a problem, talk it over with a grown-up you trust.
- And every once in a while, give yourself a pat on the back and say, "I'm one cool kid!"
  (This one is my favorite.)

Tina Truly

It's Quiz Time!

Here's a fun test I made up to see how well you understand the whole responsibility thing.

1. **If you want a pet, you should:**

   A. start calling your little sister Sparky.
   B. prove you're responsible by doing a great job with your other chores.
   C. learn how to make balloon animals.

2. **Responsible kids:**

   A. eat liver and spinach every night.
   B. consider what other people need or expect from them.
   C. live on the planet Dutycalls.

3. **Being careless with your things:**

   A. means that sometimes you have to live with broken stuff.
   B. will give you a rash.
   C. makes people want to give you more stuff.

4. **When you've got a really big chore to do, you should:**

   A. look in the Yellow Pages and call a professional for help.
   B. break it down into smaller tasks.
   C. demand a raise in your allowance.

5. **Making checklists and doing things at about the same time every day are:**

   A. symptoms of Mad Gerbil Disease.
   B. two good ways to stay organized.
   C. things only adults do.

6. **Rules are:**

   A. for the birds.
   B. meant to be broken.
   C. there to help us.

7. **If you're in too many activities, you might:**

   A. get stressed out and not really enjoy them.
   B. start growing a third arm.
   C. need to hire a personal assistant.

8. **What do bike helmets, seatbelts, healthy foods, and exercise have in common?**

   A. They make you barf.
   B. They keep you safe and fit.
   C. They keep you from having any fun.

9. **If you say you're going to do something, you should:**

   A. go watch TV instead.
   B. do it.
   C. pick up the latest edition of *Excuses for Any Occasion*.

10. **Which of these statements is true?**

    A. Lots of problems can be solved by thinking creatively.
    B. You're the only one in the whole world who has problems.
    C. If you have a problem, you should ignore it and hope it goes away.

Answer Key:

1-B, 2-B, 3-A, 4-B, 5-B, 6-C, 7-A, 8-B, 9-B, 10-A

From My Personal Hero File: George Washington

Being responsible isn't easy. Sometimes you have to put aside what YOU want and do what's best for your family, or your friends, or your community. Even your country. That's what George Washington did. I learned about George on a TV show the other night and thought his story would go well with today's column.

George Washington was born in Virginia a long time ago. It was 1732—I just looked it up. At that time, the United States wasn't even a country yet. It was a colony of Great Britain's and had to follow British laws. Many of the colonists, including George, thought those laws weren't fair.

People thought George was a good soldier. He was smart and confident and really listened to all the facts before he made any big decisions. In 1775, George was elected head of the American army. It took eight hard years of fighting, but finally George and the colonists beat the British. Some people liked him so much they wanted to make him king! (He said, "No thanks.")

At that point, George really wanted to go home and devote himself to farming. But the brand-new country needed help. George couldn't just walk away. He stayed involved in Virginia politics and helped organize the Constitutional Convention in 1787. That was when our whole government kind of came together. George was elected the first President of the United States. He had lots of ideas about what the president's role should be. We still follow those ideas today.

By the time George finished his second term as president, the new government was doing okay, and he went back to his home, called Mount Vernon. He died three years later. Some people who study history think that without George's sense of responsibility, the United States would never have made it. At least, it wouldn't be the way it is today.

Wow. Where would we be right now if George had decided to stay home rather than to serve his country? Now there's something to think about.

Words to Know

Here's a list of some words that are good to know. Go ahead, read it. It'll help you remember all the stuff we talked about.

advice column—a feature in magazines and newspapers (and in this case, a book!). People write in with questions, and some really smart person called a columnist writes back with answers.

consequences—the end result of what you do or don't do. Like, if you keep teasing your brother when your parents told you to stop it, the consequence is that they'll get mad, and you might get no dessert or something.

crab—what you call a person who's really, really cranky. When you think about it, crabby people do look kind of like crabs. Their eyes bug out a little, and you get the feeling they'd like to reach out and pinch you.

credentials—experiences that show that a person has what it takes to do a certain job

impress—to make someone think that you're really great. Like, last week when I did the laundry without having to be asked, I totally impressed my parents.

irresponsible—the opposite of being responsible. Trust me, being called irresponsible is NOT a compliment.

lectures—speeches that go on and on, and people just have to listen

Mad Gerbil Disease—Okay, you got me. I made this one up, totally. You have nothing to fear from your gerbils, unless they crawl up the legs of your pants and tickle you until you can't stand it anymore.

mature—to act in a sensible, grown-up kind of way. (Not that all grown-ups are mature. Sometimes kids are more mature than adults.)

responsibility—So, like, that's what this whole book has been about. You tell me what it means. (Hint: Think about keeping promises, taking care of your things, being on time, and stuff like that.)

schedule—a definite plan of events or things to do. Schedules can include lots of things, from dental appointments to sleepovers to school conferences to washing the windows. (Schedules don't HAVE to be written down, but I don't recommend doing things that way, unless you've got the world's best memory.)

To Learn More

At the Library

Coville, Bruce. *The Prince of Butterflies*. San Diego: Harcourt, 2002.

Graves, Keith. *Pet Boy*. San Francisco: Chronicle Books, 2000.

Raatma, Lucia. *Responsibility*. Mankato, Minn.: Bridgestone Books, 2000.

On the Web

FactHound offers a safe, fun way to find Web sites related to this book. All of the sites on FactHound have been researched by our staff.

1. Visit *www.facthound.com*
2. Type in this special code: 1404800301
3. Click on the FETCH IT button.

Your trusty FactHound will fetch the best sites for you!

Index